WHAT MAKES A GOYA A GOYA?

Richard Mühlberger

The Metropolitan Museum of Art
Viking

NEW YORK

VIKING

First published in 1994 by The Metropolitan Museum of Art, New York, and Viking, a division of Penguin Books USA Inc., 375 Hudson Street, New York, New York 10014, U.S.A. and Penguin Books Canada Ltd., 10 Alcorn Avenue, Toronto, Ontario, Canada M4V 3B2.

Produced by the Department of Special Publications, The Metropolitan Museum of Art
Series Editor: Mary Beth Brewer
Production: Elizabeth Stoneman
Front Cover Design: Marleen Adlerblum
Design: Nai Y. Chang
Printing and Binding: A. Mondadori, Verona, Italy

Library of Congress Cataloging-in-Publication Data
Mühlberger, Richard. What makes a Goya a Goya?/Richard Mühlberger. p. cm.
ISBN 0-670-85743-2 (Viking)
ISBN 087099-720-3 (MMA)
1. Goya, Francisco, 1746–1828—Criticism and interpretation—Juvenile literature. 2. Painting, Spanish—Juvenile literature. [1. Goya, Francisco,1746–1828. 2. Painting, Spanish. 3. Art appreciation.] I. Title.
ND813.G7M74 1994 759.6—dc20 94-18108 CIP AC

10 9 8 7 6 5 4 3 2 1

ILLUSTRATIONS

Unless otherwise noted, all works are by Francisco Goya.

Pages 1 and 2: *Bullfight in a Village*, oil on canvas, 17³/₄ x 28³/₈ in., 1812–15, Real Academia de Bellas Artes de San Fernando, Madrid; photograph, Giraudon/Art Resource, New York.

Page 6: *Self-Portrait*, red chalk on paper, 7⁷/₈ x 5⁵/₈ in., The Metropolitan Museum of Art, Bequest of Walter C. Baker, 1971, 1972.118.295.

Page 8: Diego Velázquez, *Juan de Pareja (b. ca. 1610, d. 1670)*, oil on canvas, 32 x 27¹/₂ in., The Metropolitan Museum of Art, Purchase, Fletcher Fund, Rogers Fund, and Bequest of Miss Adelaide Milton de Groot (1876–1967), by exchange, supplemented by gifts from friends of the Museum, 1971, 1971.86.

Page 9: Giovanni Battista Tiepolo, *The Apotheosis of the Spanish Monarchy*, oil on canvas, 32¹/₈ x 26¹/₈ in., The Metropolitan Museum of Art, Rogers Fund, 1937, 37.165.3.

Page 10: *The Crockery Vendor*, oil on canvas, 102 x 86⁵/₈ in., 1779, All rights reserved, © Prado Museum, Madrid; photograph, Erich Lessing, Art Resource, New York.

Page 13: *Don Manuel Osorio Manrique de Zuñiga (1784–1792)*, oil on canvas, 50 x 40 in., The Metropolitan Museum of Art, The Jules Bache Collection, 1949, 49.7.41.

Page 15: *Goya in His Studio*, oil on canvas, 16¹/₂ x 11 in., ca. 1790–95, Real Academia de Bellas Artes de San Fernando, Madrid.

Page 16: *The Duchess of Alba*, oil on canvas, 82⁵/₈ x 58³/₄ in., 1797, Courtesy of The Hispanic Society of America, New York.

Page 18: *The Swing*, point of brush, gray wash on paper, 9³/₈ x 5³/₄ in., The Metropolitan Museum of Art, Harris Brisbane Dick Fund, 1935, 35.103.2.

Page 19: *Back to His Forebear*, from *Los Caprichos*, aquatint, 8¹/₂ x 5⁷/₈ in., 1799, The Metropolitan Museum of Art, Gift of M. Knoedler & Co., 1918, 18.64(39).

Page 19: *The Sleep of Reason Produces Monsters*, from *Los Caprichos*, etching and aquatint, 1799, 8¹/₂ x 5⁷/₈ in., The Metropolitan Museum of Art, Gift of M. Knoedler & Co., 1918, 18.64(43).

Page 20: *The Family of Charles IV*, oil on canvas, 110¹/₄ x 132¹/₄ in., 1800, All rights reserved, © Prado Museum, Madrid.

Page 23: Diego Velázquez, *Las Meninas*, oil on canvas, 125¹/₄ x 108⁵/₈ in., 1656, All rights reserved, © Prado Museum, Madrid.

Pages 24–25: *Bullfight in a Village*, oil on canvas, 17³/₄ x 28³/₈ in., 1812–15, Real Academia de Bellas Artes de San Fernando, Madrid; photograph, Giraudon/Art Resource, New York.

Page 26: *Spanish Entertainment*, lithograph, 11⁷/₈ x 16¹/₈ in., 1825, The Metropolitan Museum of Art, Rogers Fund, 1920, 20.60.3.

Page 26: *Pepe Illo Making the Pass of the "Recorte,"* from *La Tauromaquia*, etching, burnished aquatint, drypoint, and burin, 9¹/₂ x 13³/₄ in., The Metropolitan Museum of Art, Rogers Fund, 1921, 21.19.29.

Page 26: *The Forceful Rendon Stabs a Bull with the Pique, from Which Pass He Died in the Ring at Madrid*, from *La Tauromaquia*, etching, burnished aquatint, and burin, 9⁷/₈ x 13³/₄ in., The Metropolitan Museum of Art, Rogers Fund, 1921, 21.19.28.

Page 27: *The Agility and Audacity of Juanito Apiñani in the Ring at Madrid*, from *La Tauromaquia*, etching and aquatint, 9⁵/₈ x 14 in., The Metropolitan Museum of Art, Rogers Fund, 1921, 21.19.20.

Page 28: *The Burial of the Sardine*, oil on panel, 32⁵/₈ x 24³/₈ in., 1812–14, Real Academia de Bellas Artes de San Fernando, Madrid.

Page 33: *The Colossus*, oil on canvas, 45⁵/₈ x 41³/₈ in., 1808–12, All rights reserved, © Prado Museum, Madrid.

Page 34: *Giant*, aquatint, 11¹/₄ x 8¹/₄ in., by 1818, The Metropolitan Museum of Art, Harris Brisbane Dick Fund, 1935, 35.42.

Page 35: *And There is Nothing to Be Done*, from *Disasters of War*, etching, drypoint, burin, and lavis, 5¹/₂ x 6⁵/₈ in., 1810–14, The Metropolitan Museum of Art, Harris Brisbane Dick Fund, 1932, 32.62.17.

Page 35: *Nor This*, from *Disasters of War*, etching, aquatint, burnishing, drypoint, and burin, 6¹/₄ x 8¹/₈ in., 1810–14, The Metropolitan Museum of Art, Rogers Fund, 1922, 22.60.25(36).

Page 36: *The Third of May, 1808*, oil on canvas, 104³/₄ x 135⁷/₈ in., 1814, All rights reserved, © Prado Museum, Madrid.

Page 40: *The Forge*, oil on canvas, 75¹/₄ x 47⁵/₈ in., ca. 1812, Copyright The Frick Collection, New York.

Page 41: *Gravediggers*, brush and brown and gray-brown wash on paper, 8¹/₈ x 5⁵/₈ in., 1817–20, The Metropolitan Museum of Art, Harris Brisbane Dick Fund, 1935, 35.103.32.

Page 42: *Self-Portrait with Doctor Arrieta*, oil on canvas, 45¹/₂ x 31¹/₈ in., 1820, The Minneapolis Institute of Arts.

Pages 44–45: *The Witches' Sabbath*, oil on canvas, 55¹/₈ x 172¹/₂ in., 1821–23, All rights reserved, © Prado Museum, Madrid.

Page 46: *The Witches' Sabbath*, oil on canvas, 17³/₈ x 12¹/₄ in., 1797–98, Museo Lázaro Galdiano, Madrid; photograph, Scala/Art Resource, New York.

Page 47: *Self-Portrait*, brush and gray wash on paper, 9³/₁₆ x 5¹¹/₁₆ in., 1795–1800, The Metropolitan Museum of Art, Harris Brisbane Dick Fund, 1935, 35.103.1.

Page 49: *The Letter*, oil on canvas, 71¹/₄ x 49¹/₄ in., Musée des Beaux-Arts, Lille.

CONTENTS

SELF-PORTRAIT
*This self-portrait was a study for the opening illustration in
the first of Goya's great series of prints, Los Caprichos.*

Meet Francisco Goya

Francisco José de Goya y Lucientes was born on March 30, 1746, in the village of Fuendetodos. His home was located in a desolate region of northern Spain, where winds howl during bitter-cold winters and the heat parches the landscape in the summertime. At the time of Goya's birth, his father, who had been trained as a gilder, farmed a small piece of land. When Goya was a young child, he and his family moved about twenty miles away to Saragossa, the capital city of the Aragón province. There his father returned to the craft of gilding.

Goya attended a religious school, and his best friend there, Martín Zapater, remembered him as "a restless and turbulent" companion. In 1760, Goya became apprenticed to José Luzán, a respected painter in Saragossa. He spent three years working with Luzán, then in 1763 went to Madrid, the capital of Spain. Goya's growing talent was soon observed by another artist from Saragossa, Francisco Bayeu, who taught at the Royal Academy of San Fernando, the national art school. Bayeu was also court painter to the king of Spain, and he chose Goya to be an assistant in his studio at the palace. Working with Bayeu prepared the young Goya for his own career. In the royal palace, he could see the great art that kings had collected through the centuries from many parts of the world.

It was the art of Diego Velázquez, the great Spanish painter of the previous century, that inspired Goya most. He admired the natural way in which Velázquez painted. His realism was unsurpassed in its day. Perhaps Goya also coveted the position the artist had held as court painter. Goya eventually was awarded the post himself.

When Goya arrived in Madrid, important painting projects usually went to foreign artists. Giovanni Battista Tiepolo, Italy's leading artist at the time, was painting a splendid, light-filled mural on the ceiling of the palace's throne room. Goya learned from everything he saw, but to complete his education he had to travel abroad.

In 1763 and again in 1766, Goya entered the Royal Academy's competition for a travel scholarship. Both times he lost, but finally, in 1770, he traveled to Italy on his own. When

Diego Velázquez
JUAN DE PAREJA
Goya admired Velázquez more than any other artist. Here Velázquez's subject is at ease, not stiff and formal. The brushwork is free, yet gives a realistic impression. Goya sought to return to this native Spanish naturalism.

Goya returned from his trip, Bayeu arranged for the young man's first commission, decorating the ceiling in Saragossa's cathedral. As Goya gained experience, he collaborated with Bayeu, who never ceased to help him. In 1773, Goya married Bayeu's sister, Josefa. Soon afterward, he became an independent artist.

Goya and the Age of Reason
Goya lived during the time of the French Revolution, when European society challenged the power of kings. Spain was old-fashioned and resisted the changes that were sweeping through Europe. But it was Goya, a Spaniard, who witnessed a bloody war against foreign invaders in his own country and recorded those turbulent, horrifying events in powerful and original ways.

All his life Goya suffered from illness, which eventually left him deaf. It may have been this infirmity that prompted him to look deep inside himself for ideas. Although Goya's images can be brutally realistic, they can also be fantastic and dreamlike. Other aspects of his character are equally contradictory.

Goya relished his position as court painter, yet his art often criticized political rulers and religious and social institutions. It was injustice and superstition—the absence of reason—that Goya blamed for the disasters he saw all about him. Goya was a man of his time, which has been called the Age of Reason. His art brings to life the light of reason as well as the dark monsters that hide inside the minds of human beings.

Giovanni Battista Tiepolo
THE APOTHEOSIS OF THE
SPANISH MONARCHY

This study for a ceiling painting by Tiepolo shows the kind of art the king desired for his palace. Tiepolo painted a woman in the center who represents the Spanish monarchy rising toward heaven, conveying the idea that the Spanish king belonged among the gods. This light and airy look was typical of the eighteenth-century style called Rococo, of which Tiepolo was a master. By the time Goya became a court painter, the Rococo style already seemed old-fashioned.

The Crockery Vendor

One of Goya's first commissions for the palace was a series of tapestry designs. In this work of 1779, three women sit on the side of the road inspecting crockery. The young man sprawled out before them offers pots for sale. Goya's lively design makes it clear that the women, not the crockery vendor, are the subject of the painting. The elbow of the man in red is aimed directly at them, and their heads are centered within the great blue arc of the wheel. The circular design of the wheels repeats the shapes of the gleaming ceramics, and so do the bales of hay on which the people sit. Even the sleeping dog is curled into a rounded shape. Goya saved his brightest yellow for the shawl of the woman closest to the viewer, drawing attention to her wide-eyed face.

Other artists of the time also painted scenes showing everyday activities, but Goya was unique in the liveliness he gave his subjects. Here he added a little drama that is universally understood. The vendor in the lower left gestures to the young woman in yellow. He seems ready to leave his work to take her away with him.

Goya's painting is eight and a half feet high and was copied, full size, in silk and wool threads by weavers at the Royal Tapestry Works. During a period of sixteen years, Goya painted more than sixty of these large cartoons, as designs intended for copying are technically called. More than

once, the artist was asked to simplify his designs and tone down his hues, for his radiant colors and intricate details were a break with tradition.

Royal Appreciation

Goya's modern approach celebrated the labors and fiestas of his countrymen. The tapestry woven from this design was hung, along with several others based on Goya's cartoons, in the bedchamber of Prince Charles and Princess María Luisa. The prince so admired Goya's work that he honored the artist by asking him to show four cartoons to the royal family before they were delivered to the tapestry factory.

Goya made the woman sitting inside the gilded coach stand out by framing her face against the bright yellow sky. One of the men with his back to the viewer wears a brilliant red coat, and the tilt of his head leads to the woman. She is the only person in the painting who looks directly out at the viewer.

Don Manuel Osorio Manrique de Zuñiga

Before long, the most powerful people in Spain knew of Goya. In 1785, he was appointed deputy director of the Royal Academy of San Fernando, the school that had rejected him as a youth. By 1786, he had become one of the official painters to the king.

One of Goya's patrons was the count of Altamira. Goya painted portraits of several members of the count's family, including his son Manuel. Here the family's importance is conveyed in the fine lace that trims the boy's bright red suit, the satin sash tied around his waist, and his well-crafted white shoes.

Goya placed the boy in the middle of the canvas. Light enters the picture from the left, creating large areas of light and dark that frame the child and emphasize his doll-like stature. He

stands in the brightest area. Next to Manuel is a domed cage filled with finches, which gather at the bottom of the cage, some hopping to higher perches. Manuel holds a string in his hands that is tied to a magpie. But danger lurks: Behind the magpie, three cats stand ready to pounce. The cats are partly in shadow, the one farthest back almost merging with the dark wall behind him. Only his big eyes and raised ears are visible. This darkness makes the cats seem sinister.

Lessons Through Symbols

In Goya's time, moral lessons were often told through symbols. The count may have wanted the menacing cats and the vulnerable birds to appear in the portrait of his son as reminders that innocence is constantly threatened by cruel nature.

Goya's composition is symmetrical, with the cats and the cage taking up about the same amount of space on either side of Manuel. This use of symmetry balances the left and right sides of the composition, and also contrasts two ideas, captivity and freedom.

The leashed magpie lifts a business card from the floor and holds it in his beak. The card is decorated with a picture of an artist's tools and, in elegant script, the name Goya, showing that the painter was the humble servant of his patron.

EL Sr D.ⁿ MANVEL OSORIO MANRRIQ.^e D ZVÑIGA S.^r DE...

Goya in His Studio

According to his son, Goya "painted only in one session, sometimes of ten hours, but never in the late afternoon. The last touches . . . he gave at night by artificial light." This explains the odd hat the artist wears in this self-portrait.

When Goya worked at night, he wore a special hat equipped with metallic pincers, into which candles could be placed. The artist would have had to stand very close to the canvas to get much help from their light!

This painting is set in daytime, and light floods through the studio window, eliminating many of the room's details. The light forms a halo around the painter, who gazes intently out at the viewer.

No Rules in Painting

Goya's regard for the art of painting was very great, yet he publicly insisted that "there are no rules in painting." Details of this intimate view of his Madrid studio show that his claim was only partly true. The unusually clean palette, with dabs of paint neatly arranged, proves that he knew good studio practice. He also knew the correct way to balance a palette against his left hand and forearm while grasping extra brushes in his free fingers. Another detail shows that Goya broke rules when he knew a better way of doing something. He painted the light without the help of a brush, the conventional method of applying paint. Instead, he scraped the paint on with a palette knife. Sometimes he even applied paint with his fingers.

There may have been a practical purpose to Goya's exaggerated illumination. Looking at paintings by candlelight was a favorite activity of the nobility, and Goya knew that in such dim surroundings, his brilliant light would seem like real daylight entering the viewing room. The light coming through the window is blinding in its intensity, while in other areas of the painting, it is subtler. Across the artist's back and legs, light dissolves shadows, making the body look three-dimensional. The delicate point of light on the desk and the blending of light and shadow on the wall under the window bring a sense of real atmosphere to the painting.

Light has a symbolic meaning, too. Because it comes from above, light has often been linked to the divine. In art it sometimes represented the power of God. By surrounding himself in this heavenly light, Goya shows that his art is inspired from above.

Despite Goya's air of confidence here, it was at about this time that he became deaf. This terrible reverse in his life was the result of a mysterious but grave illness. He was forty-seven years old and was never to hear again.

Goya controlled light effects in his small self-portrait so that his head and torso are silhouetted but not flattened. His dark leggings, set against dark shadows, appear rounded because of the light that touches them.

The Duchess of Alba

The dark silhouette of a woman stands out boldly against an empty sky, her face framed by cascading hair and a headdress. In the center of the composition, a thin, elegant hand points emphatically to the ground. Unlike the woman's face, the hand reveals more than it hides. On it are two rings. The larger of them, on the middle finger, is engraved with the woman's ancient and noble family name, Alba. The second, on the forefinger, carries the name Goya.

Goya's Powerful Friend

The woman is the duchess of Alba, who, after the king and his family, was one of the highest-ranking nobles in Spain. She was outstanding not only for her wealth and rank, but also for her beauty and charm. Although Goya was sixteen years her senior, they became close friends, and she was his frequent model.

Here she wears a bold red sash, which, together with the gold of her bodice and sleeves, emphasizes her slender elegance. The brilliant colors stand out dramatically against the black of her gown.

Costumed as a *Maja*

Goya painted this portrait of the duchess a year after her husband's death, but her black garments are not a sign of mourning. Like many of her

wealthy contemporaries, she is wearing the latest fashion, which was a kind of masquerade. At the time, lively young people who lived in the poor neighborhoods of Madrid escaped the boredom of poverty by promenading up and down the finest streets of the city. These men and women, dubbed *majos* and *majas*, respectively, attracted attention with their gaiety and the simple elegance of their costumes. The garments of a *maja* included a full black skirt, a tight bodice,

The words Solo Goya *were once covered by paint applied by either Goya or someone else later on. Only the duchess and Goya knew what the inscription really meant.*

and a traditional black veil, known as a *mantilla*, that fell over the shoulders from a high comb worn in the hair. The duchess imitated the fashion, but her elegant shoes and jewelry and her ornate gold sleeves make it clear that she is not poor.

In this painting, a clue suggests that Goya and the duchess may have been in love. She points down to an inscription in the sand, *Solo Goya*, which means "only Goya." Although the duchess died just five years later, Goya must have cared for her deeply, since this picture remained with him in his studio until his own death.

In 1799, Goya advanced to the highest position a Spanish artist could hold, first painter to the king. Delighted at his prestigious new post, he bragged to his boyhood companion, Martín Zapater, saying, "The king and queen are mad about your friend Goya."

THE SWING

Colorful young people, always dressed alike, delighted the upper classes with their spirit and vivacity. Goya used a gray wash to quickly picture this frivolous couple.

BACK TO HIS FOREBEAR   THE SLEEP OF REASON PRODUCES MONSTERS

Goya pictured many kinds of folly in the celebrated series of etchings entitled
Los Caprichos, *meaning "whimsies," which was published in 1799. They
could be hilariously funny as well as terrifying. The left image,* Back to His
Forebear, *shows an ass taking pride in his family heritage. His ancestors
were "asses," too! Here Goya pokes fun at aristocratic snobbery. On the
right, in* The Sleep of Reason Produces Monsters, *Goya illustrates the
potential evil within man's imagination when reason is abandoned.*

19

The Family of Charles IV

In 1800, King Charles asked Goya to come to the palace at Aranjuez to paint a group portrait of his family. The painting that resulted marks the high point of Goya's role as first painter to the king.

Clustered in three groups, Spain's royal family stands here casually in a large gallery as if waiting to pose for Goya. While the family members wait, their eyes scan the room, which is full of paintings. Although they are in their own home, they seem uncomfortable, strangers to the place and its decorations.

Goya pictured thirteen members of the royal family. On the left side of the painting is a self-portrait of the artist, who is shown preparing a huge canvas for the group portrait he is about to begin.

A Royal Gathering

The center of the canvas is occupied by Queen María Luisa, wife of Charles IV, the king of Spain. She has decorated her hair, ears, and neck with jewelry, and pulls her daughter close to her. The bright red suit worn by her youngest son, who stands next to her, draws the viewer's eyes to the middle of the canvas.

On the right stands Charles IV, wearing four shining, star-shaped medals, which cover his large chest and stand out against his black suit. His sixteen-year-old son, Prince Ferdinand, stands to the left dressed in blue. The prince's twelve-year-old brother hides shyly behind him, hanging on to his waist.

Piecing Parts Together

It is very unlikely that the royal family ever stood together like this for Goya to paint them. He executed hundreds of portraits in his lifetime, and many of them were of the king and queen, whose faces he must have known by heart. He painted ten studies from life of other family members before he began the group portrait, a large canvas that took him almost a year to complete. Goya was an expert at composing from sketches and recollections, piecing the parts together so that they appeared to be freshly observed.

The king wanted everyone to be shown in court finery. Fancy costumes, jewelry, and sashes and medallions, all symbols of honors bestowed by the king, could easily lead to stiff, formal poses. To avoid this, Goya decided to picture the

Goya paid tribute to Velázquez by painting himself in a group portrait of the royal family of Spain. Goya is on the left in the shadows behind his canvas.

family members as though they were just gathering in the room he was using as a studio.

While Goya carefully observed the family from life, he also looked to the most celebrated portrait of the Spanish court, *Las Meninas*, painted in 1656 by his hero, Velázquez. As Velázquez had done, Goya included himself in the picture, and showed the family informally. Whereas in *Las Meninas* the family appears warm and engaging, in Goya's painting the figures seem stiff, cold, and unfriendly. The queen casts an imperious glance, while the others barely look at one another. It is hardly conceivable that Goya would create an intentionally unflattering picture of the royal family, but it was the last time he painted them, although he remained in their service for many more years.

Diego Velázquez
Las Meninas
Velázquez included himself, but all the attention is on the little princess. The title of the painting refers to the ladies-in-waiting who surround her.

Bullfight in a Village

Stubbornly planting all four hooves in the dust, a defiant bull dares the picador to move closer. To make the animal prominent, Goya painted it in profile and set it against the sunbaked sand. By slightly turning the bull's head, he showed both of its eyes, alert to the surrounding commotion. The circle of onlookers, schooled in the drama of the fight, are ready for action. Bright light and dark shadows suggest an early afternoon hour.

"Picador" comes from the Spanish word that means prick or pierce, which describes the picador's role in the bullfight. From his well-trained horse, this character carefully aims his lance at the bull. His goal is to weaken the bull's neck so the matador can move in for the kill. The matador, partly hidden by the head of the horse, appears with his legs spread in the same stance as the bull's, but he is poised to leap away should the bull charge. Goya muted the color of the bullfighter's "suit of lights," an outfit brightly ornamented to attract the bull. A blue cape, bunched up in the matador's right hand, will attract a charge when it is flapped near the bull's lowered head. Eventually, the bull and the matador will come face to face. Rushing in on the left, a young man is about to attempt a flying leap over the animal's shoulders.

The colors of earth and sky—reddish brown, black, blue, and white—and touches of red are

the only colors Goya used to capture the small-town bullfight. This painting was done on wood, a common substitute for canvas and used for small pictures. Fine black lines delineate some of the figures, such as the horse, the man running toward the bull, and the seated man on the wall in the lower right corner of the painting. The brushstrokes are loose and free, giving the impression of movement and action.

A Symbol of Life

The bullfight was of great importance in Spain, not just as a sport but as a rite. The bull represented death, and the matador was a symbol of life. Goya himself was a tremendous fan, and he executed a series of prints of bullfighting scenes. But this painting incorporates more than just Goya's interest in the subject. It was one of five scenes of everyday Spanish life he painted in the 1810s, all on wood panels. Unlike the royal family, who commissioned his official work, nobody paid Goya to paint these pictures. He did them to explore his own personal interests. *Bullfight in a Village* shows that Goya was not afraid to portray brutality when he saw it in real-life events, and that he could also capture the energy of such moments.

BULLFIGHTS

Goya devoted an entire series of prints to bullfighting, Spain's national sport. The lively action of men and animals was a subject of endless variety.

The Burial of the Sardine

This is another of Goya's pictures on wood panel depicting a scene of everyday Spanish life. As in *Bullfight in a Village*, he shows a great spectacle, with a crowd of people in a circle. Late afternoon sun spotlights the white gowns and upraised arms of the dancers. Smiles and rosy cheeks mask the faces of the two women clad in white, while the disguise of a hag obscures the identity of the third performer. Their audience is enthralled, and several people approach from the edge of the circle. A crouching figure in the black costume of a bear lunges toward the women from the left. Another, dressed as the devil and wearing a mask in the form of a human skull, imitates a dancer from behind.

A Defiant Celebration

The title of the painting, *The Burial of the Sardine*, implies a mock funeral, but it is only a figure of speech. It refers to the fast from meat observed during Lent in Roman Catholic countries like Spain. The plentiful but unpopular sardine was the least expensive substitute for meat. Anticipating this dull, unappealing diet, people held fiestas at which they enjoyed roast pigs and other rich foods. On Ash Wednesday, before the penitential fast began, and in defiance of Church tradition, there was a celebration in which the sardine was mocked, or "buried."

Goya views this celebration from on high so that no one blocks the scene. At the same time, he shifts his vantage point to get behind some of the couples in the front row. One pair naps in each other's arms, while the woman next to them applauds. Her partner hugs her, and points to the performers. In the corner of the painting, a mother helps her small child understand what is going on.

The banner, decorated with a huge grinning mask and held high in the middle of the crowd, sways back and forth just like the dancers. The triangle at the bottom of the banner is almost the same size as the one formed by the space between the women in white, linking the two areas. As in *Bullfight in a Village*, the brushstrokes are loose and free, conveying the exuberance of the scene.

The Colossus

Looming over the horizon and clothed only in billowing clouds, a giant treads the countryside. Light washes across his chest and shoulder, while dark shadows cloak his back and forearm. Goya used a dramatic contrast of light and dark to increase the haunting quality of the monster, partially hiding the colossus behind the horizon to make him seem even more mysterious. Goya's painting may represent the giant's birth as he emerges from the earth.

Although the colossus is walking away from the valley below, he frightens a large caravan. Wagons, riders, and cattle are arranged in columns as if they were leaving a town in orderly fashion. Suddenly, fear and terror begin to grip the people and the animals. A frenzy of bulls stampedes in one direction, while horses and people race the other way. One man falls off his mount and a woman collapses. Panic spreads everywhere. Goya suggests a large, horrified crowd without defining details. Most of the figures are represented by little more than small strokes of paint. The tilt of each figure tells whether the person is running, falling, or frozen in fear. To increase the ominous effect, Goya painted the top and the bottom of his picture

Goya used few colors and little detail in the animals and people frightened by the colossus.
Gestures and postures describe their frantic attempts to escape from the unknown.

GIANT

Goya liked to explore the same images in many ways. In this print, he shows the colossus at rest.

jet black. The top gives the impression of a heavy curtain descending from above, while the bottom seems to roll toward the valley like a wave.

The Spirit of Spain

Some say *The Colossus* represents the spirit of Spain rising up against the foreign troops that entered Madrid in 1808. Born of Spanish soil, this giant moves forward, fists raised to fight for the people below, unaware that they are frightened by his hulking presence.

The occupation of Spain was ordered by Napoleon Bonaparte, the famous military leader who rose during the revolution that rid France of its hereditary king and queen. Many Europeans, including Goya, supported Napoleon, believing that he favored liberty and progress. Opinions changed in 1804, however, when Napoleon crowned himself emperor; his ambition was to rule all of Europe.

Napoleon forced the Spanish royal family into exile and, in 1808, put his own brother on the throne. Goya remained court painter, but in his private works he bitterly and brilliantly observed the effects of war on his country, capturing the suffering in a series of etchings called *The Disasters of War*. These scenes showed that nightmares easily could become reality during wartime.

AND THERE IS NOTHING TO BE DONE

Goya learned etching and other printing processes so he could produce his designs in large numbers and distribute them to others. The Disasters of War *is a series of prints of scenes that are full of grim and savage reality. Goya believed war was blind to right and wrong, so symbols of blindness occur in many of his designs. Here gun barrels are shown, but not the faces of the soldiers who hold them. The man they are about to shoot is blindfolded. The foreground execution is repeated farther back in the composition, against a background of black smoke.*

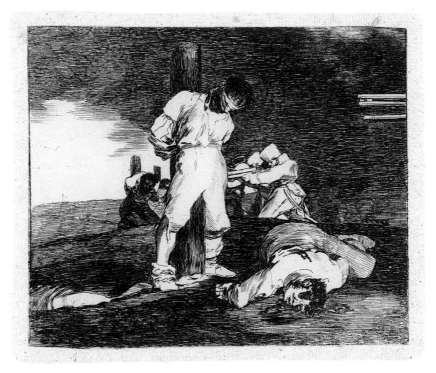

NOR THIS

This terrible scene of war is set against a dark sky that is penetrated by rays of light. The foreign soldier who looks at the dead man with indifference has probably killed so many people that it has become routine to him.

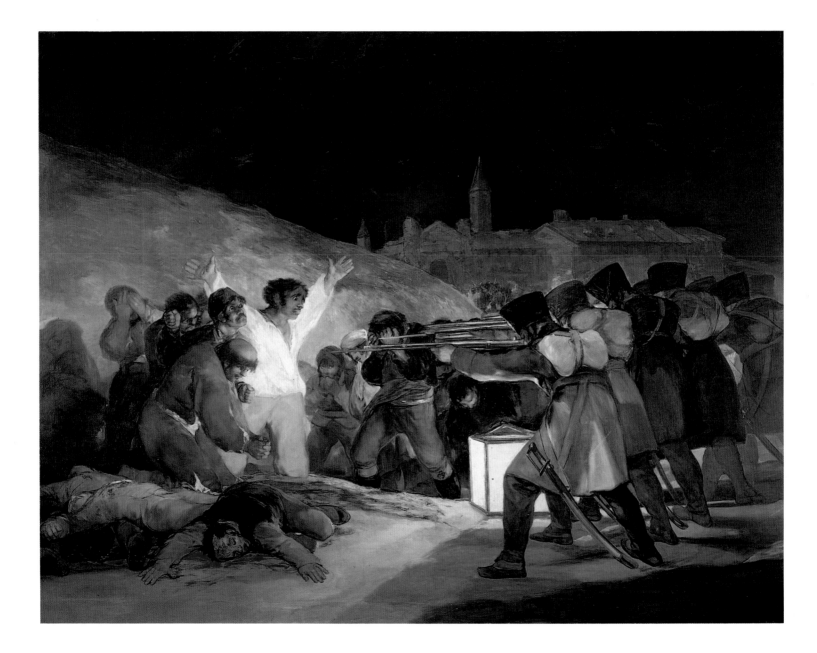

The Third of May, 1808

Goya expressed his reactions to the war in his country not only through his etchings, but also in large-scale paintings. In 1814, after the war had ended, he painted *The Third of May, 1808*. In the past when artists chose war as a subject, they celebrated its triumphs. Goya instead chose to portray its brutal and senseless violence.

Against a stark, hilly backdrop, Goya showed a French firing squad executing Spanish countrymen during the night. The artist made one man symbolic of all the others: the figure dressed in pure white and yellow, who, with his arms up, is about to be shot. His bright clothing stands out against the muted browns, blacks, and blues of the night. His pleading eyes are wide with terror. Beneath him are the bloody bodies of the men who have already been killed, one of them with his arms spread out, echoing the pose of the standing man in white. Around the central figure, comrades react: Some pray, while others recoil in despair, covering their faces with their hands. To the right, more men huddle, knowing that they, too, will soon be dead.

Forming a diagonal line, the French soldiers stand firmly, pointing their guns. Goya illustrated their uniforms and their military gear but refused to show their faces, making the soldiers seem anonymous and cold-blooded. In contrast, the artist made the painting's focal point the face of the man who is about to be shot, whose gesture of surrender, with arms spread out, evokes the image of Christ on the cross.

Goya's painting is based on an actual event. When Napoleon's troops entered Madrid on May 2, 1808, outraged citizens, armed only with knives, rose up against them. The next evening, these Spaniards were executed by the French on Príncipe Pío hill, which is included in this painting. Goya depicted the events that occurred to commemorate the Spanish spirit, but he does not glorify war. In this painting the victims, not the victors, are the real heroes. Goya created a picture that transcends time and place, one that remains today among the most brilliant war paintings ever made.

The Forge

Goya shows blacksmiths forging a piece of metal. The heads, arms, and torsos of the three tightly grouped men reveal their intense involvement, practiced rhythm, and perfect coordination. Goya pictured them from below eye level, as though he were looking up at them. This vantage point makes the figures seem monumental, as does the size of the canvas, which is almost six feet tall. The blacksmith with the white shirt spreads his legs, bends his knees, and lifts his hammer over his head, preparing to deliver a blow to the object being fashioned on the red-hot anvil. The young laborer opposite him holds the object in place, aided by the senior smith.

By emptying the blacksmith's shop of the usual tools and supplies, Goya allowed the room to serve as a gray frame around the three men. He did not include many details in this painting. Late in his life, the artist said, "My eye never sees outlines or particular features or details. . . . My brush should not see better than I do." With broad brushstrokes, he simplified the men's hair, skin, and clothes, as well as the metal, and designed a compact composition that highlights the concentration and skill of the blacksmiths.

A Celebration of Power

Unlike the images of everyday life Goya had created for his tapestry cartoons more than thirty years earlier, this scene is not a lighthearted entertainment. Here the artist presents these working men in a monumental way, celebrating their power. This picture may, in fact, refer to the forging of the new Spanish constitution of 1812.

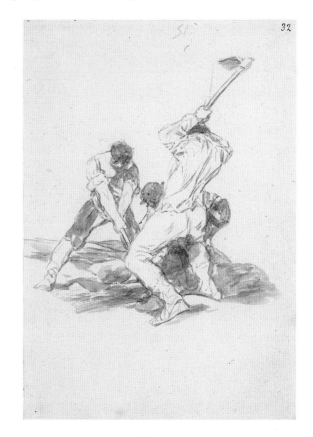

GRAVEDIGGERS
Goya's drawing in brown and gray wash of men digging may have been a point of departure for The Forge.

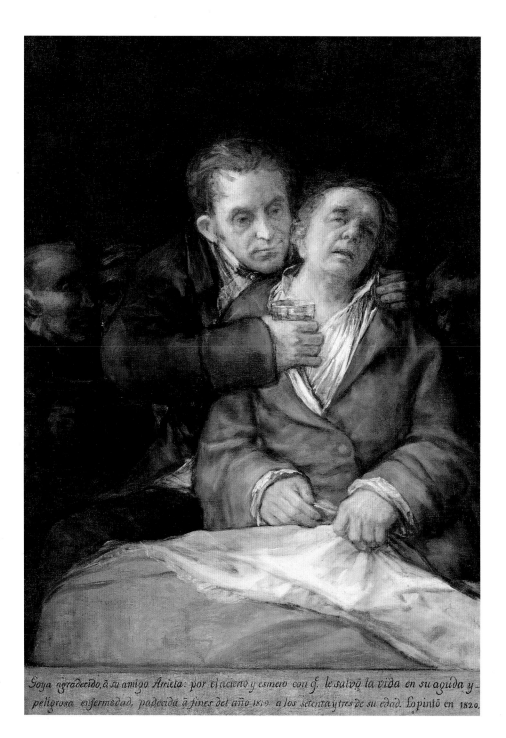

Goya agradecido, á su amigo Arrieta: por el acierto y esmero con q.ͤ le salvó la vida en su aguda y peligrosa enfermedad, padecida á fines del año 1819, a los setenta y tres de su edad. Lo pintó en 1820.

Self-Portrait with Doctor Arrieta

Toward the end of 1819, Goya suffered a violent recurrence of the disease that had earlier plagued him. Through the help of his compassionate doctor, he survived his illness. A year later, the artist pictured the event in this double portrait.

Barely able to sit, Goya slumps into the arms of Doctor Arrieta. The artist's disheveled white shirt frames a pale, exhausted face, but also emphasizes the steady hand of the doctor, who gently coaxes his patient with a glass of medicine or water. As he resists the doctor, Goya leans back in semiconsciousness.

The faces of the two men almost touch. The doctor's clear brow, deep-set eyes, and steady gaze show that he is concentrating on his patient with devotion and kindness. In the background, whispering ghostlike figures hover over the artist and his physician.

A Grateful Memory
The bright red of the bedcover directs attention to the bottom of the painting. An inscription there reads, *Goya in gratitude to his friend Arrieta: for the skill and care with which he saved his life during his acute and dangerous illness, suffered at the end of the year 1819, at the age of 73. He painted this in 1820.* Goya fabricated this highly personal and unusual double portrait from a grateful memory.

Although in the past Goya, along with others, had poked fun at incompetent doctors, here the artist elevated Arrieta to an almost religious height. By showing his compassion as well as his knowledge of the science of medicine, Goya made him a redeemer.

Some have speculated that the shadowy figures in the background of this painting are friendly servants. Others suggest that they are demons of death, waiting for Goya's soul.

The Witches' Sabbath

In the middle of the night, dozens of witches huddle closely together in a terrible swirl. In the foreground at left sits a goat shrouded in the robes of a monk. He must be their leader, in the role of Satan. Sitting apart from the crowd on the far right, a lone *maja* recoils.

Goya defines faces, feet, and bent bodies in loosely rendered brushstrokes, capturing each

expression in quick notations. Eyes bulge, necks twist, fingers twiddle, toes stick out from under skirts, and shoulders surge back and forth.

Goya knew about witch lore, and in the 1790s, he featured witches in six paintings commissioned by noble patrons. About twenty years later he executed this enormous painting of a familiar subject for himself. Goya had bought a country house near Madrid that was handsomely situated on a river, with groves of trees all around it. Before long, the villa was a retreat he seldom left, and it became known as the Quinta del Sordo, or "deaf man's house." Two large rooms, one upstairs and one downstairs, were reserved

THE WITCHES' SABBATH

In comparison to the sinister mystery of the "Black Painting," this earlier version of the same subject is almost playful.

imagination. Known as the "Black Paintings" for their somber colors and disturbing subjects, these works include *The Witches' Sabbath*. When they are experienced all together, they seem like images from a house of horrors. Years after Goya's death, they were moved from the Quinta del Sordo to Madrid's Prado Museum.

"I Keep Learning"

Convinced that his modern ideas might get him into trouble in his native Spain, Goya hid for a time, then moved to France in 1824. A friend described him as "deaf, old, awkward, and weak, but very desirous of seeing the world." The artist visited Paris first, then settled and continued working in the Bordeaux region, where other Spanish exiles lived. Across the bottom of one of his last drawings he wrote, *I keep learning*. Goya died on April 16, 1828.

Goya proudly named his most important teachers. The first was Velázquez; the second was Rembrandt, Holland's greatest artist. The third was nature. Velázquez showed Goya how great a Spanish court artist could be. Rembrandt showed him that an artist could look inside himself to tell stories that had universal meaning. Nature showed him all the rest. But Goya did not list the special thing that made him great, because it was so much a part of himself: his imagination. He had an inner vision that saw what others never did. He also had the generosity to share his vision with others through his art.

for a special project. Compelled by images in his mind's eye, Goya painted directly on the walls. In less than five years, he completed fourteen frightening compositions, charged with his macabre

SELF-PORTRAIT

What Makes a Goya

Some of Goya's favorite subjects were scenes from everyday Spanish life.

His paintings are filled with quick, loose brushstrokes.

Goya loved black.

Goya liked to paint women dressed in the traditional Spanish costume of a *maja*.

He only roughly indicated the background.